CELEBRATING
MID-AUTUMN FESTIVAL

Celebrating Mid-Autumn Festival

EUGENIA CHU & Y.Y. CHAN

Illustrated by Eliza Hsu Chen

Celebrating Mid-Autumn Festival

Paperback ISBN: 978-1-7334808-8-8
Hardcover ISBN: 978-1-7334808-7-1

Library of Congress Control Number: 2023910654

Illustrated by: Eliza Hsu Chen

https://eugeniachu.com
https://www.yychani.com

To my Brandon—as always
Eugenia Chu

To my students
Y. Y. Chan

CONTENTS

WHAT IS THE MID-AUTUMN FESTIVAL?

Mid-Autumn Festival, also called the Moon Festival or the Mooncake Festival, is one of the most important holidays in Chinese culture, second only to Chinese New Year. Similar holidays are celebrated in other countries in East and Southeast Asia. In Mandarin Chinese the Mid-Autumn Festival is called Zhōngqiū jié (中秋节).

Zhōngqiū jié (中秋节) dates back over 3,000 years and traditionally falls on the 15th day of the 8th month of the Chinese **lunisolar calendar**[1] when the moon is believed to be at its fullest. This is usually in September or early October on our calendar, known as the **Gregorian calendar**. In ancient times, people **worshiped** the moon in autumn to thank it for the **harvest**. Today people celebrate it as a time for family reunions.

[1] The lunisolar calendar is based on the movements of the sun, the moon and the seasons so the Mid-Autumn Festival falls on a different day each year, usually in September or October.

HISTORY AND FOLKLORE

The term 'Mid-Autumn' first appeared in 475-221 BC. However, the term was only used to describe the time and season, as the festival didn't exist yet.

The Mid-Autumn Festival, or Zhōngqiū jié (中秋节), originated from the **custom** of Chinese **emperors** worshiping the moon during the Zhou Dynasty (1050-221 BC). They believed the practice would bring them a plentiful harvest the following year. Early customs involved offering **sacrifices** to the moon.

During the Tang Dynasty (618-907 AD), the custom of appreciating the moon became popular among the upper class. It wasn't until the Northern Song Dynasty (960-1279 AD) that Zhōngqiū jié (中秋节) was officially established on the 15th day of the 8th **lunar month**.

Zhōngqiū jié (中秋节) became increasingly popular during the Ming Dynasty (1368-1644 AD) and the Qing Dynasty (1644-1912 AD). It was as popular as Chinese New Year!

The Mid-Autumn Festival became a Chinese public holiday in 2008. This day is usually connected with the weekend to make it a three-day holiday in China.

The Mid-Autumn Festival was once Valentine's Day in ancient China.

THE LEGEND OF HOUYI AND CHANG'E–THE MOON GODDESS

There are various **myths** and **legends** surrounding the Mid-Autumn Festival, but the most well-known is the story of *Houyi* (后羿) and *Chang'e* (嫦娥). Here is one version of this popular myth.

In ancient times, ten suns circled Earth. One day, all ten appeared together, setting Earth on fire. *Houyi* (后羿), a brave archer, took down nine of them, saving the planet. As a reward, the Jade Emperor, Ruler of Heaven, gave him an **elixir of immortality**—but only enough for one person. He took it home but chose not to drink it because he did not want to become immortal without his beloved wife, *Chang'e* (嫦娥). However, one day when *Houyi* (后羿) was away, his **apprentice** broke into his house to steal the magical potion. To keep him from stealing it, *Chang'e* (嫦娥) drank the elixir herself. Soon after, she flew to the moon, where she became its goddess.

Houyi (后羿) was heartbroken when he figured out what happened to *Chang'e* (嫦娥). He shouted to the sky and found that the moon was especially bright that night. He saw a swaying figure that looked just like *Chang'e* (嫦娥). To show how much he loved and missed her, *Houyi* (后羿) laid out *Chang'e's* (嫦娥) favorite fruits and cakes, beginning a tradition of preparing a feast in her honor on this day every year.

On the next Mid-Autumn Festival, look to the night sky to see if you can spot *Chang'e* (嫦娥) gazing down on us!

THE TALE OF THE JADE RABBIT

According to one version of this folklore, three
immortals turned themselves into poor old men. They
begged for food from a fox, a monkey, and a rabbit. The
fox and monkey gave them food, but the rabbit did not
have anything to share. The rabbit felt so bad that he
offered himself as a meal and jumped into the fire. The
immortals were so touched by the rabbit's sacrifice that
they sent him to the moon to become the eternal jade
rabbit. Since then, the Jade Rabbit (*Yùtù* 玉兔) has lived
on the moon and has been *Chang'e's* (嫦娥) companion.

The Jade Rabbit (*Yùtù* 玉兔) also makes medicine for those living in Heaven to remain immortal. Can you see him on the moon?

PREPARATION

The roundness of the moon represents unity and family reunion. Preparing for *Zhōngqiū jié* (中秋节) is like planning a big reunion dinner party, similar to Thanksgiving celebrated in the United States. It helps to plan in advance by:

1. Picking the location;
2. Setting the menu;
3. Inviting family and friends;
4. Buying or making **mooncakes**, called *yuèbǐng* (月饼);
5. Decorating.

Mooncakes, or *yuèbǐng* (月饼), are the main event! They symbolize the moon and family unity. The cake is traditionally cut into pieces that equal the number of people in the family. They are enjoyed as part of the celebration and are also given as gifts prior to the festival. You can buy mooncakes from most Chinese bakeries or Asian grocery stores. You can also buy them from Amazon or make your own using the recipes at the back of this book! The most traditional flavor is lotus seed paste with salted duck egg yolk inside, but you can fill them with anything you like—even chocolate! Yum!

Some families have dinner at a restaurant while others dine at home with family and friends. Afterward, they go out to gaze at the moon while enjoying yummy *yuèbǐng* (月饼).

As with most festivals, it is always fun to decorate! Lanterns are the most popular way to liven up a Mid-Autumn Festival party. They are easy to find and you can even make your own, like the ones in this book! Some people write wishes on their lanterns for things like health, love, good grades, and good fortune, while others write riddles.

Some families also honor **ancestors** during this festival by burning candles and **incense**.

YOU ARE WHAT YOU EAT

Every family in every region serves different foods, but here are a few common dinner dishes:

1. Mooncakes—*yuèbǐng* (月饼), of course!

2. Roast pork—represents strength and health.

3. A whole chicken—represents happiness and health, and serving it whole symbolizes completeness and family unity.

4. Crab—hairy crab is a seasonal **delicacy** and special for this feast.

5. Duck—relates to a folk tale[2].

6. Lotus Roots—symbolizes strong family bonds.

7. Pear—ensures reunion and prevent separation.

8. Taro—symbolizes warding off evil spirits and brings good luck and wealth.

9. Round fruits like pomelos, apples, Asian pears, grapes, melons and peaches; symbolize family unity and togetherness, like the moon.

10. Fall's harvest like pumpkin, chestnuts, taro, persimmons, sweet potato, walnuts, and mushrooms.

² In the 14th century, the people in Northern China were battling the enemy who were called *Dázi* (韃子) which sounds like *yāzi* (鸭子), the word for duck. The people used the code "eat duck" for a secret mission that overthrew the enemy during the Mid-Autumn Festival of 1338. Since then, eating duck during the Mid-Autumn Festival has become the custom in many places.

POPULAR MOONCAKES

- Lotus seed paste mooncakes with salted egg yolks
- Ham & nut mooncakes
- Red bean paste mooncake
- 5 kernel and roast pork mooncake
- Shanghai savory mooncake
- Pineapple mooncake
- Snow skin mooncake
- Nutella/chocolate mooncake
- Green tea mooncake
- Ice cream mooncake
- Cream cheese mooncake
- Seafood mooncake

HOW TO CELEBRATE

ADMIRING THE FULL MOON

T he tradition of gazing at the moon dates back to the Zhou **Dynasty** (500 BC) when people held ceremonies to welcome the full moon. These days, people go outdoors after the family reunion dinner to admire the full moon on the night of the Mid-Autumn Festival.

EATING MOONCAKES– YUÈBǏNG (月饼)

The tradition of eating *yuèbǐng* (月饼) began during the Yuan Dynasty (1279-1368 AD), which was ruled by Mongols. The mooncakes were actually used to pass around messages to rebel against the Mongols at the time. Nowadays, families and friends usually share a mooncake on the night of the Mid-Autumn Festival.

PLAYING WITH LANTERNS

Making and lighting up lanterns is another popular tradition of the Mid-Autumn Festival, or *Zhōngqiū jié* (中秋节). Lighting lanterns is a symbol of hope and good luck. There are many different ways to make a lantern, but the most common method involves using colored paper or silk and bamboo sticks. Some lanterns are designed to be carried on the end of a long bamboo stick, while others are hung in trees or outside houses and buildings. Sometimes they are floated on rivers to create a festive atmosphere. Of course, it is important to dispose of or recycle all waste!

Children enjoy making their own colorful lanterns in different shapes to resemble animals, plants, or flowers.

During the festival, they carry them while parading around the neighborhood. See the Culture Corner section for instructions on how to make lanterns using paper plates or tissue paper.

LANTERN RIDDLES

People can write riddles on the lanterns for others to guess the answers. Lantern riddles, called *dēng mí* (灯谜), are an important part of *Zhōngqiū jié* (中秋节), as they reflect the values and traditions of Chinese history and culture. The riddles are usually short and clever. They often contain puns, wordplay, and cultural references based on poems, folklore, historical events, or jokes about social issues.

This tradition is over 1,500 years old. It is still popular today as it is a great way to exercise your brain and bond with family and friends. Lantern riddles are not only entertaining but also educational, as they promote language learning, critical thinking, and cultural awareness.

AROUND THE WORLD

O ther countries and regions of China have unique traditions.

For example, in Hong Kong, you can watch fire dragon dances where 300 people parade a 220-foot dragon lined with sticks of incense from head to tail! There are also traditional lion dances where two dancers inside a lion costume jump and dance to entertain the crowds. Everyone enjoys festival foods, drinks, and lantern displays, too.

Singapore, Malaysia, and the Philippines have many **ethnic** Chinese citizens. Their celebrations are similar to those in China, such as lighting lanterns and dragon dances. However, while celebrated on the same day as in China, it is not a public holiday.

In Japan, the main customs for *Tsukimi* or *Otsukimi* ('moon-viewing') include offering sacrifices to the moon and celebrating the harvest. During the festival, residents wear their national clothes. They carry the shrine to the temple where they burn incense. Children collect reeds to decorate doors, symbolizing good luck and happiness.

In Vietnam, *Tết Trung Thu* is a traditional festival mainly for children. Parents buy their children various types of lanterns, snacks, and funny masks. The main activities include worshiping the God of Earth, carrying carp-shaped lanterns, and watching a lion dance parade.

In Korea, *Chuseok* is one of the biggest holidays. Koreans traditionally travel back to their hometowns to spend time with their families, feast, and pay respect to their ancestors. South Koreans typically sweep the tombs of their ancestors one or two days before the Mid-Autumn Festival. The eldest son worships their ancestors first, and then the family dances together to show appreciation for the moon. Young girls wear colorful traditional clothes. And everyone gathers to play folk games like *talchum* (mask dance), *ganggangsullae* (Korean circle dance), and *ssireum* (traditional Korean wrestling).

The full moon does not always appear on the Mid-Autumn Festival night!

CULTURE CORNER

T he Mid-Autumn Festival is an even more special occasion when people participate in its many fun activities. Try these at home with family and friends:

- Mooncake Recipes

- Paper Lanterns

- Lantern Riddles

- Dice Game

MOONCAKE RECIPE

Mid-Autumn Festival is all about the mooncakes, or *yuèbǐng* (月饼), so of course we had to include a simple recipe for you to try! Everything you need can be found on Amazon.

Makes: 6 mooncakes
Cook time: 15-20 min.
Prep time: 40-50 min.

What you'll need: mooncake mold; flour sifter; parchment paper; plastic wrap

---

3 tbsp golden syrup
1 cup cake flour (plus extra for dusting)
¼ tsp lye water

2 tbsp vegetable oil
6 tbsp (6 oz) lotus seeds paste
1 egg (beaten)
Salted egg yolks (optional)

1. Mix the golden syrup, lye water, and vegetable oil.
2. Sift the flour and add to the above mixture.
3. Mix with a fork (or hands) until it becomes a soft dough.
4. Put the dough on plastic wrap and refrigerate for 30 min.
5. Separate the lotus seed paste into 6 equal parts and roll into balls.
6. Dust the mooncake mold with flour.
7. Separate the dough into 6 equal parts and roll into balls.
8. Flatten a ball of dough and wrap it around a ball of lotus seed paste.
9. Roll to form a ball and put it in the flour-dusted mooncake mold.
10. Plunge the piston of the mold down to form the shape of the mooncake.
11. Bake on a parchment-lined tray/pan for 5 min. at 350°F.
12. Remove from oven and brush the tops with egg to glaze, then dab with napkin to remove excess.
13. Bake for another 10-15 min. at 350°F or until golden brown.
14. Remove from the oven, cool, then eat!

15. For a softer consistency, store in an airtight container for 3 days.

For an even more traditional mooncake, add a salted egg yolk to each mooncake. If you don't like lotus seed paste, replace it with your favorite filling like red bean paste or chocolate—yum!

SUPER EASY ICE CREAM MOONCAKE RECIPE

Makes: depends on mold
Cook time: 40 min.
Prep time: less than 5 min.

What you'll need: silicon mooncake mold (available on Amazon)

Dark chocolate melting wafers
Your favorite ice cream

1. Melt the chocolate for a few seconds in the microwave or stovetop.
2. Coat the mooncake molds with the melted chocolate.
3. Place in the freezer for 5-10 min. until the chocolate hardens.

4. Fill the mold with ice cream.

5. Cover the ice cream with more melted chocolate.

6. Freeze for at least 30 min. until solid.

PAPER LANTERNS

Making paper lanterns is so fun! Finish one and hang it somewhere special, or make a bunch and hang them everywhere! Don't forget to write riddles on them for the Lantern Riddles game (see page 28).

Here are two easy lantern crafts you can try!

Tissue Paper Lantern

Rubber balloons	LED light
Tissue paper or toilet paper	Scissors
White glue	String (16 in.)
Water	Tape
Paintbrush	Bamboo/wooden stick
Pressed leaves and flowers	

1. Mix the glue with some water (1:1 ratio).
2. Blow up the balloon to your desired size and tie the opening.
3. Use the paintbrush to apply glue to the balloon and add some tissue paper to it. Continue until the whole balloon, except its opening, is covered.
4. Put some pressed leaves and flowers on top then apply more glue over that.
5. Add one more layer of tissue paper with glue to cover the leaves and flowers.

6. Leave it overnight for everything to dry.

7. Use scissors to deflate the balloon, then take it out of the lantern.

8. Cut around the opening and punch two holes on opposite sides to loop the string through. Then tie a knot at the end of the string and tie the string around the end of the stick to make the handle.

9. Switch on the LED light and place it inside the lantern. Tape it down.

10. Hang the lantern wherever you want or carry it with the handle.

11. Optional: Attach lantern riddles on the bottom of the lanterns with tape. See Lantern Riddles on page 28 for examples.

Paper Plate Lantern

6 paper plates	Tape
4 paper lace doilies	Glue
Colored paper and markers	Stapler
2 pieces of yarn or string	Scissors
(16 in. each)	Craft knife
Bamboo/wooden stick	LED light

1. Cut out a circle in the middle of one paper plate. This will be the top of the lantern. Then, cut four small, equally apart openings on the paper plate frame for the lantern strings.

2. To make the lantern's four sides, cut out a circle in the middle of the paper plates. Next, glue a paper lace doily over each circle opening and wait for them to dry.

3. Use colored paper to decorate the lantern sides. You can cut out different shapes and glue the pieces onto the lantern or just draw on the plate and add decorations.

4. Staple all the plates together to form a box. One non-cut plate is for the bottom of the lantern, one with the circle cut out is for the top, and four plates with the lace doilies glued on are the sides. The bottom of the plates should face inside.

5. To make the lantern handle, take two pieces of yarn or string and tie four knots on the ends of each piece. Pull the knots through the four openings of the top lantern plate and attach the strings to a wooden stick with tape.

6. Switch on the LED light and place it inside the lantern, then tape it to the bottom.

7. Hang the lantern up or take it out for a stroll!

8. Optional: Attach lantern riddles on the bottom of the lanterns with tape. See Lantern Riddles on page 28 for examples.

LANTERN RIDDLES

Lantern riddles, or *dēng mí* (灯谜), are riddles written on lanterns or slips of paper attached to lanterns. The lanterns are then hung in public places such as parks or temples for people to admire and solve.

Examples of lantern riddles:

1. What is full of holes but still holds water? (A sponge)
2. What is always in front of you but can't be seen? (The future)
3. What has a head and a tail but no body? (A coin)
4. Sometimes it's curved like a smile, other times, it's round like a plate. (The moon)
5. What goes up but never comes down? (Age)

Question formats for your own riddles:

1. What has...but cannot/doesn't...?
2. What is...but...?
3. Why...

Now you are ready for the Lantern Riddle Game!

Solving lantern riddles is a fun way to pass the time during the festival, and it is a popular activity for families and friends to do together. Those who solve the riddles correctly may win a small prize!

Lanterns with riddles
Prizes

1. Prepare a master list of all the riddles with the correct answers. Then hang the lanterns in a visible area and number them.
2. Players may guess the answers, individually or in a group. The goal is to solve as many riddles as possible before the end of the game. The host can provide some hints, if necessary, and limit how many hints are given per player.
3. Players can mark their answers with the corresponding lantern number. Then the host can check the answers using the master list at the end of the game.
4. Award prizes to the player(s) who solved the most riddles correctly. Prizes can be anything from small trinkets to gift cards or even a mooncake.

DICE GAME

Bóbǐng (博餅) is a traditional Mid-Autumn Festival dice game that dates back to the 1600s! It is believed a Chinese general invented the game to boost the morale of his homesick troops during the Mid-Autumn Festival.

Six dice
Bowl

Prizes (lots and lots of prizes— traditionally 63 prizes!)

1. Roll the dice.

2. Win a prize based on the dice combinations shown on the next page.

3. Each player rolls once per turn until all the prizes have been given out.

4. If a die rolls out of the bowl, you lose your turn.

Prize	Dice Results	Example
1st Place	Six of the same;	
	Five of the same except 4;	
	Four 4s	
2nd Place	Straight— 1, 2, 3, 4, 5, 6;	
	Two sets of trios (three of the same)	
3rd Place	Four of any number besides 4	
4th Place	Three 4s	
5th Place	Two 4s	
6th Place	One 4	

LEARN TO SAY IT!

Here are a few common phrases people say to each other during the Mid-Autumn Festival:

Zhōngqiū jié kuài lè!

中秋节快乐!

HAPPY MID-AUTUMN FESTIVAL!

Zhù nǐ hé nǐ de jiā rén zhōngqiū jié kuài lè!

祝你和你的家人中秋节快乐!

WISHING YOU AND YOUR FAMILY A HAPPY
MID-AUTUMN FESTIVAL!

Dàn yuàn rén cháng jiǔ, qiān lǐ gòng chán juān.

但愿人长久，千里共婵娟.

WISHING US LONG LIFE TO SHARE THE GRACEFUL
MOONLIGHT, THOUGH THOUSANDS OF MILES APART.

**Yuàn nǐ de shēng huó jiù xiàng zhè shí wǔ de
yuè liang yí yàng, yuán yuán mǎn mǎn.**

愿你的生活就象这十五的月亮一样，圆圆满满.

WISHING YOU A PERFECT LIFE JUST LIKE THE ROUNDEST
MOON IN MID-AUTUMN DAY.

GLOSSARY

Ancestor: a person someone is descended from and who lived several generations ago

Bóbǐng (博餅): a traditional Mid-Autumn Festival dice game

Chang'e (嫦娥): the moon goddess who drank the potion for immortality

Custom: a way of acting that is usual or accepted for a person or group

Dázǐ (韃子): 14th-century Mongolian enemy of China

Delicacy: food that is rare and delightful

Dēng mí (灯谜): lantern riddles

Dynasty: a family of rulers in a country

Elixir of immortality: a magical potion that grants eternal life

Emperor: a ruler that has total control of a country or region

Ethnic: of or relating to a group of people who share the same culture, race, or nationality

Folklore: traditional customs, tales (myths and legends), sayings, dances, or art forms preserved among a people

Gregorian calendar: the calendar most countries use (the US has been using it since 1752!)

Harvest: a mature crop

Houyi (后羿): the brave archer who saved the earth by shooting down nine suns

Immortal: gods or beings who live forever

Incense: material used to produce a fragrant odor when burned

Lunar month: the time it takes the moon to pass through all of the moon phases—about 29.5 days

Legend: a story with some basis in history and geography and tends to mention people or events

Lunisolar calendar: a calendar based on the phases of the moon (moon's orbit around the Earth), the movement of the sun (Earth's orbit around the sun), and the seasons

Mongols: people from Mongolia (a region of eastern Asia)

Mooncake: a pastry filled with sweet or savory ingredients

Myth: a symbolic story that is passed down about how or why something came to be

Sacrifice: an act of offering something precious to a deity or god

Worship: to honor or show reverence toward a divine being or supernatural power

Yāzi (鸭子): duck

Yuèbǐng (月饼): mooncake

Yùtù (玉兔): Jade Rabbit

Zhōngqiū jié (中秋节): Mid-Autumn Festival

RESOURCES

Educational websites with fun activities for kids:

MissPandaChinese.com

ChalkAcademy.com

Mid-Autumn board books/toys:

BittyBao.com/shop/p/round-4-wooden-mooncake-toy

Babysnacktime.com/products/Mid-Autumn-Moon-Festival-p465607206

Museums to visit:

New York City: Museum of Chinese in America—mocanyc.org

Washington DC: Chinese American Museum DC—chineseamericanmuseum.org

Los Angeles: Chinese American Museum—camla.org

San Jose: Chinese American Historical Museum—chcp.org

San Francisco: Chinese Historical Society of America—chsa.org

Chicago: Chinese American Museum of Chicago—ccamuseum.org

Portland: Portland Chinatown Museum—portlandchinatownmuseum.org

Seattle: Wing Luke Museum—wingluke.org

ABOUT THE AUTHORS

 **Eugenia Chu** is an attorney turned stay-at-home mom turned multi-award winning and best selling author. She is Chinese-American and lives on a magical beach in Miami with her husband, Bob, son, Brandon, and dog, Dash.

Unable to find children's story books that included Chinese language or culture when Brandon was younger, she began writing them herself. Brandon is the inspiration for all her books.

Eugenia enjoys presenting her books at schools, libraries, and festivals. She is an avid reader who delights in writing, traveling, yoga, and drinking too much coffee.

Eugenia is also the author of: *Brandon Makes Jiǎozi* (餃子); *Brandon Goes to Beijing - Běijīng* (北京); *Brandon Goes to Hong Kong - Xiānggǎng* (香港); and *Celebrating Chinese New Year*.

Visit https://linktr.ee/eugeniachu to learn more about the author and her books, or to schedule an author visit.

 **Y. Y. Chan** is a multi-award-winning children's book author based in Hong Kong. In 2020, she made a New Year's Resolution to write and publish a book and she has not looked back since. Her first two books have each received international book awards.

As a child, Chan grew up in sunny Brisbane, Australia. After graduating with First Class Honors in Primary Education, she returned to Hong Kong to teach English. She also has an M.A. in English Language Teaching and has been teaching English for over ten years.

When her father passed away, she took a break from teaching to travel, read, and write. Her writing journey began when she was tutoring and working freelance for several universities and educational publishers. She is currently teaching English at a primary school in Guangzhou, China.

When she is not writing or teaching, she is either reading or looking for more books to add to her overflowing bookshelf.

Visit www.yychani.com for more information and updates about her work.

ABOUT THE ILLUSTRATOR

 **Eliza Hsu Chen** is an illustrator and graphic designer. Born to Taiwanese parents in Brazil, she was raised in Paraguay, and then moved to Miami when she was six. Her love for art grew during her years at Design and Architecture Senior High where she majored in architecture. She received the Posse scholarship and earned a bachelors in graphic design and marketing from Syracuse University. Visit ElizaHsuChen.com to see more of her work.